Don Drumm

The Sculptor-Designer Craftsman

A pioneer of aluminum as a fine art medium,
creator of original metal sculptures
and craft pieces that enhance and complement every
household tradition.

D. A. Schafer

In thanksgiving to my husband, Paul, and our children, who supported this endeavor from the beginning.

To Pam, Jeffrey, and Mary, who helped me lay the groundwork, and have encouraged and enlightened me along this writing journey.

Bryant was my right arm throughout the editing process.

Mary Cistone, photographer for Drumm Studios, provided Drumm photographs and invaluable assistance for this endeavor.

To Lisa Drumm, who, from the very beginning, knew this story about her husband needed to be told, and believed in me to tell it.

Preface

It was a summer evening. The hall of Wadsworth Public Library, Ohio, was filled to capacity. He stood in the crowd, so unassuming. If you didn't know who to look for, you surely would not have picked him out of the assembly. The slide screen was pulled down and all awaited his arrival.

Slowly, he approached the front and stood right next to the screen and the tablet monitor. Throughout the evening, he would wrestle with the screen and challenge it to "stay put." He was so down-to-earth, we felt we were in the hands of a relative; comfortable.

Don Drumm, the maestro, began his intriguing presentation, and the pictures of his majestic artwork took us on his journey through time, challenging us to remotely comprehend the masterpieces that flashed before our eyes.

His tales about his creations, the people who revolved around his star-reaching structures, the synagogue, the mansion, the Southern town, and on and on we traveled.

Throughout these pages you will discover the man, his dreams, his stories, and his connection with his art. You will be taken to different dimensions of space, but even more than that, you will be enveloped by his heart and his passions. Sit back and let his works of art and his story bring solace and peace to your busy world.

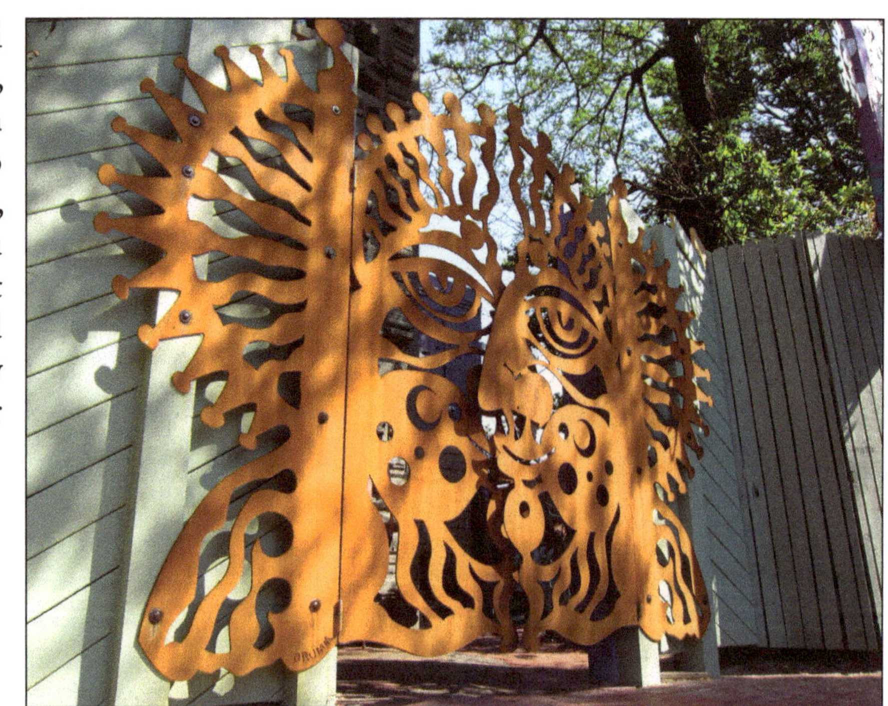

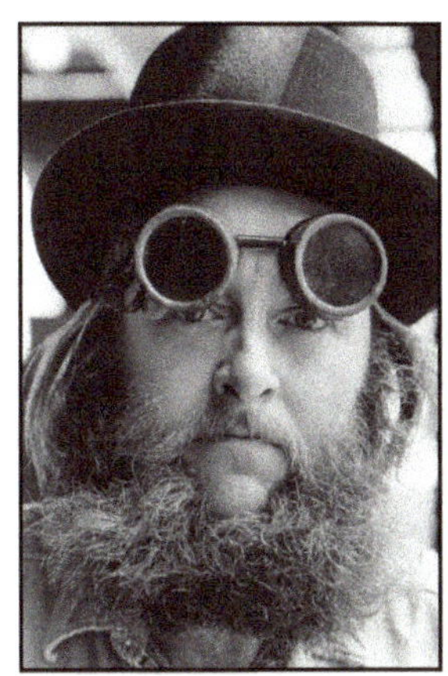

In a quiet little town in Warren, Ohio, a young man had a dream. He would create an art form that would speak for itself; he would become a master of metal art composed of steel or aluminum or stainless. This art form would find its way into every household tradition and personal taste. This art form would be free-flowing, whimsical, and occasionally even nonobjective, leaving your imagination to take over. Remember, "You are only limited by your imagination."

Art develops our senses. It expands our emotions to the limitlessness of space. To see deeply through our human conscience through a vivid piece of art is to be taken to the depth of our souls. Life has so many dimensions. Watching the trees sway in the wind can allow a rhythm to begin, a rhythm that can swallow up pain, or anger, or regret. Then, in the emptiness, peace fills the void and a gentle calm rushes in to hold and envelop you.

Metal sculpture, just like music or dance, becomes active when our minds rush to analyze it, feel it, develop an inner connection with it, possess it, feel joy from it.

Don Drumm took this unique art medium: metal, not canvas and he designed not through music notes or motion but with his mind and hands and the heat of a welding machine, forming and erecting sculptures that permeate the atmosphere with their beauty.

And so the journey goes…

While attending Hiram College to pursue a degree in premed, Don's learning was challenged due to dyslexia (a fact he discovered much later), and the opportunity to drop calculus and take on an art class became a reality. Numerous experts nurtured Don's budding talent, from Mayo Johnson to Claude Rainbolt. Each saw the genius in his work, and as teachers took him under their wings, they helped him soar. He had numerous mentors from every field: architects, business owners, CEOs, university presidents, and on and on.

These were the years of development that gave Don the stability to lead him to become artist-in-residence at Bowling Green State University. This six-year time frame developed the skills he needed to expand his horizons to Crouse Street and the building of his future studios.

Through this period, he found his soul mate and raised three incredible women who reached for their own stars and found them. Don states, "The discovery of your own destiny is a reality many often miss."

In his youth, he had worked on cars side by side with his father. Welding and tinkering, repairing, always with his hands on something. "In my senior year in high school, my dad moved us to a farm where we made stuff, but we never thought of it as art."

As Lisa put it, "Don is a design machine." Lisa chose to live in Akron, Ohio, to start her own career as an art teacher. "Akron elementary schools were the only schools in the state to offer full-time art classes." She attributes the enormous success the Drumms have realized to the sound art appreciation given in this community.

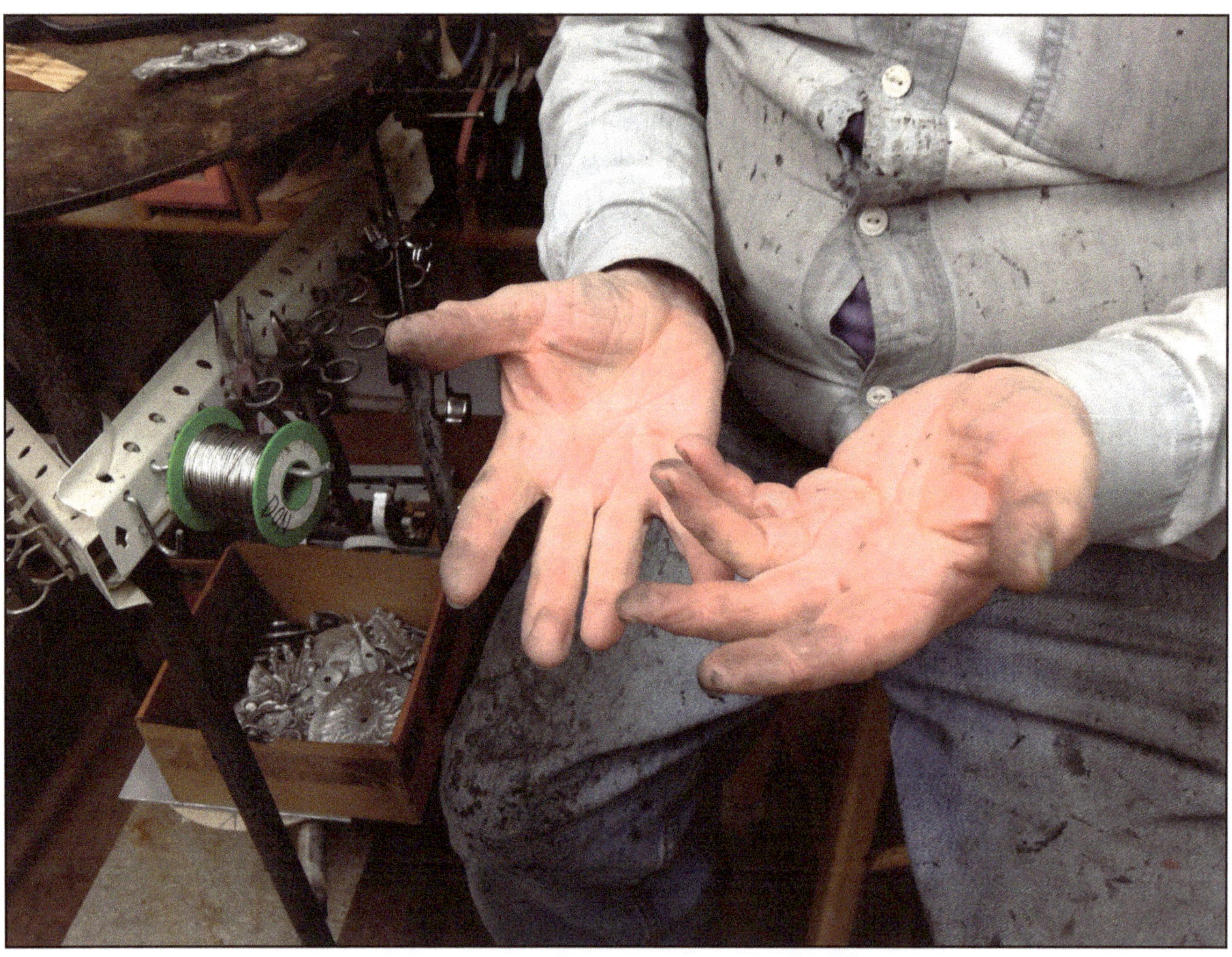

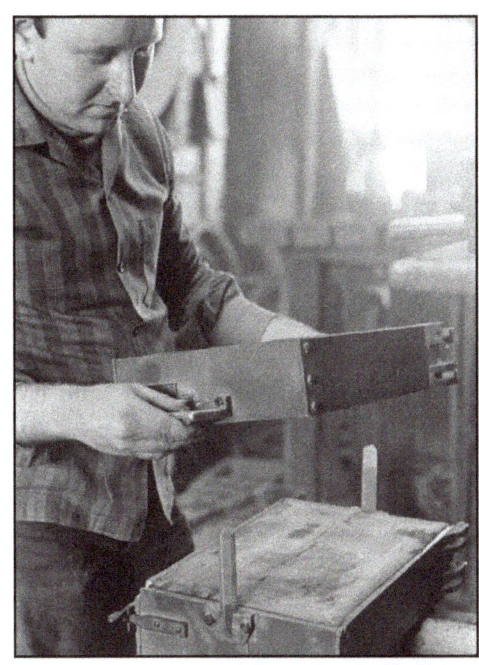

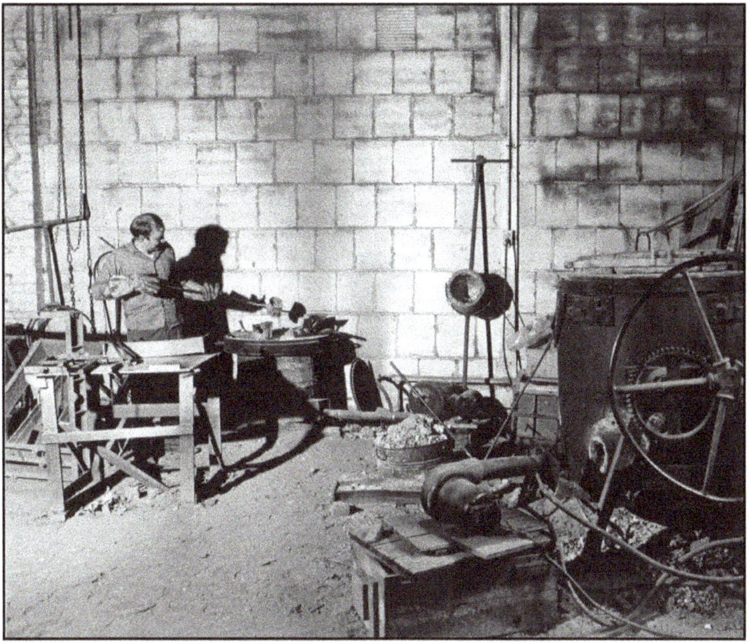

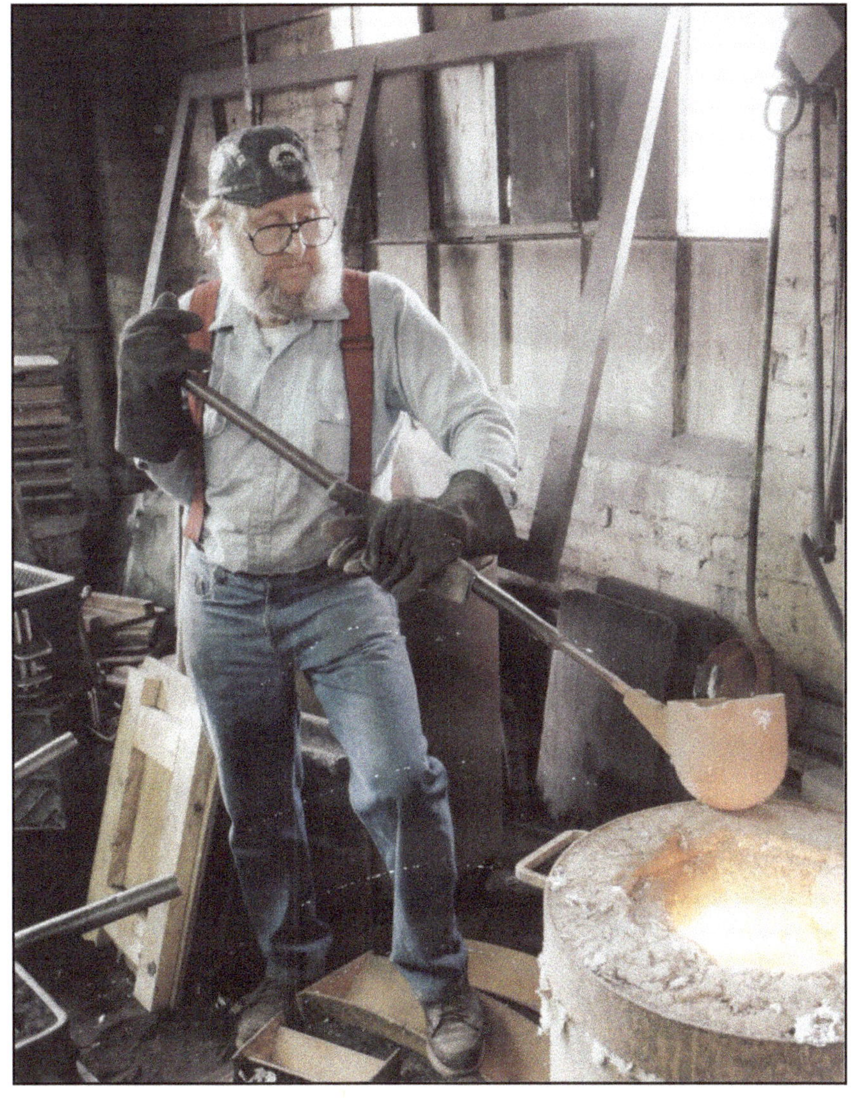

Lisa and Don are an iconic couple. They complement each other in their strengths. Don throws the ball in Lisa's court when it comes to organization and style. When Lisa took over and brought in the additional craftsmen, sales flourished, and today the organization has reached over five hundred additional artists whose works complement the Drumm collections. Don gives Lisa all the glory she rightly deserves. Lisa Drumm took hold of the running of the Gallery early on and maintains a full schedule every day with a remarkable passion for their business.

In 2016, the Drumms celebrated their forty-fifth-year anniversary of the Drumm Studios and Gallery.

Entering the Don Drumm Studios and Gallery is like walking into a rainbow. You experience such beauty and ingenuity in a maze of designs from across the globe. The Drumm art pieces reflect the incredible ingenuity of predicting what a collector would want, from clocks that mesmerize to bowls that you can picture on your dining room table overflowing with fruits or gourds or glass balls.

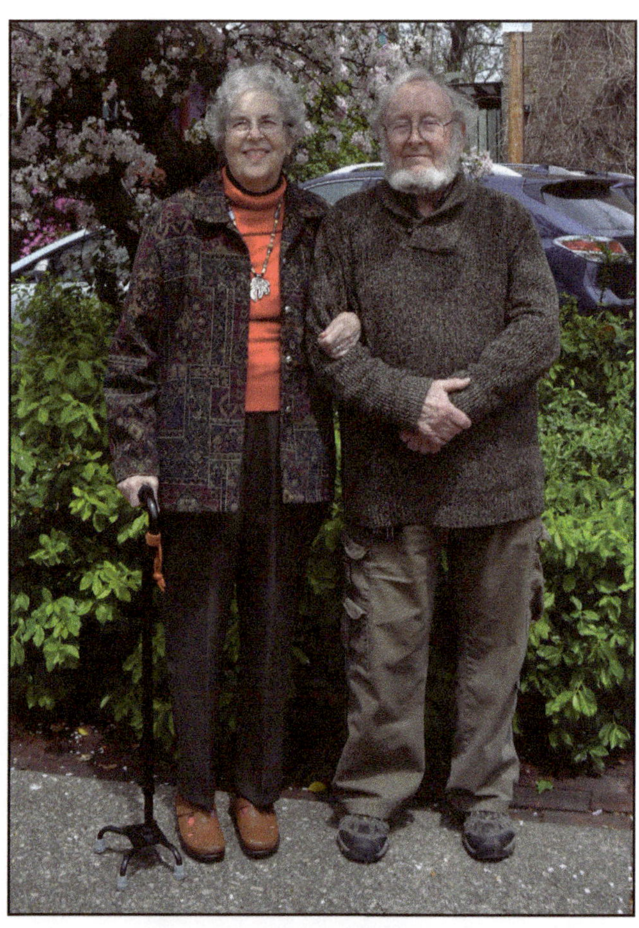

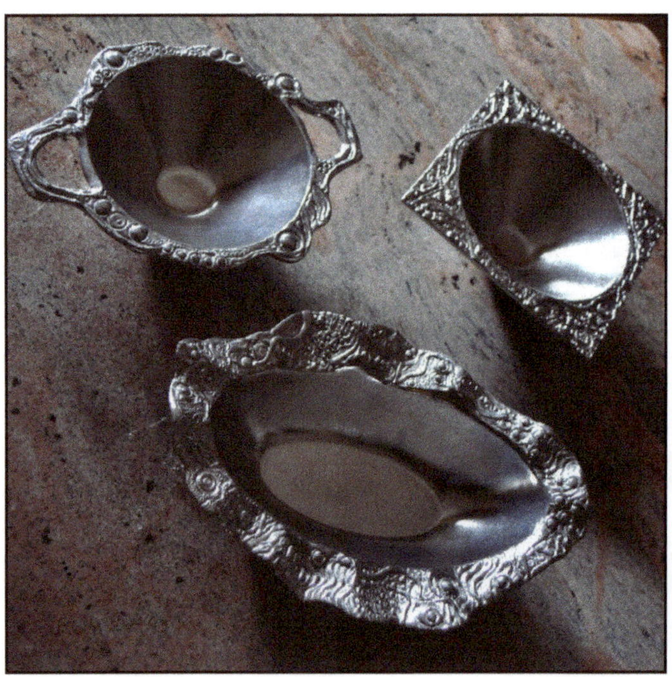

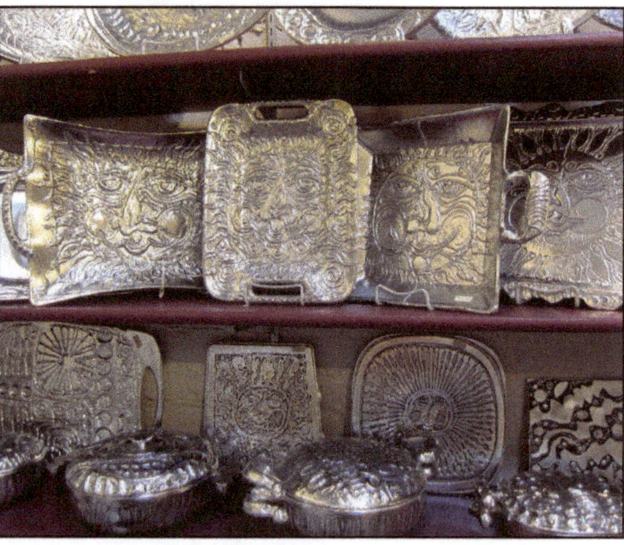

"When I was in art school, early on, one of my professors said the circle is one of the hardest shapes to deal with, because it is a complete symbol on its own. It's not broken. That intrigued me, and I used to sketch around the circle, and it evolved into a sun one day, and I forgot about the circle and continued doing the suns.

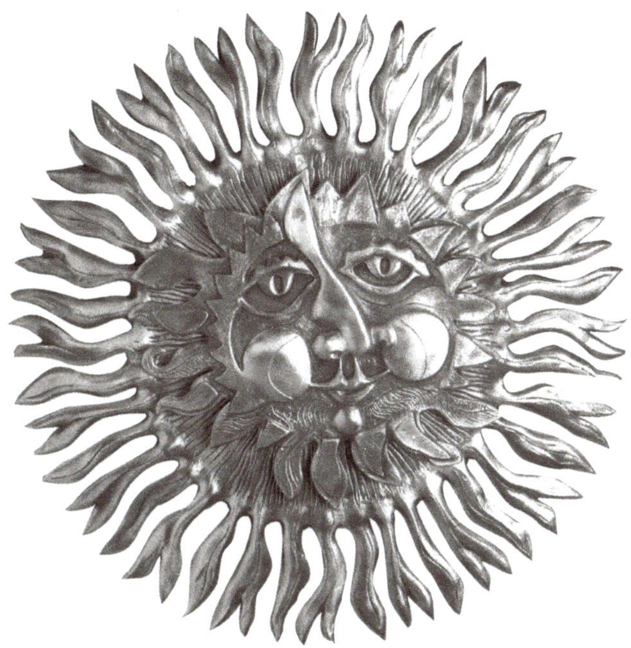

When I would do a big job in another state or big commission, it was like giving birth and having to give up the child…all the excitement of erecting something, and then it is over. You've spent a lot of time and emotion into it, and then you come back.

So then I concentrated on the sun as a way of diverting any depression. The sun was an item I could do anything with. The sun represents God. Without the sun, we wouldn't live very long. It gives us food, energy, heat, and existence. In every culture in the world the sun is a symbol of something. I enjoy doing it; each one is a little different. Everyone is probably tired of it, but I will probably do them until the time I die."

Don is an endless reservoir of determination to state his philosophy through his art. One particular large-scale piece that Don created stands two stories high in the Summa Health System's Jean and Milton Cooper Cancer Center. The piece is called Garden of Fantasy. Don states, "As I was designing it, I wanted to bring peace…A resting sense that emits power to heal."

On a personal note: I am a breast cancer survivor. Every day, the Garden of Fantasy spoke to me of overcoming the adversity as I passed it. When my treatment was complete, I asked my husband to take me to the Drumm Gallery. I had longed for a sun for years. I believed this was the time. The sun also represented the Son, shining upon me, healing me with its warmth—His warmth.

"When I start to work with a client, we start with 'What do you want to spend?' I ask them to take a picture of where they want the piece to stand. Many want me to come and visit the area, but as I have grown in my work I do not need to go as often.

"The first thing we work on is the theme and direction they want to go. They pretty much let me go with materials, design, and subject matter. I am more interested in nonobjective work.

"There are three different types of art: realism, which represents recognizable

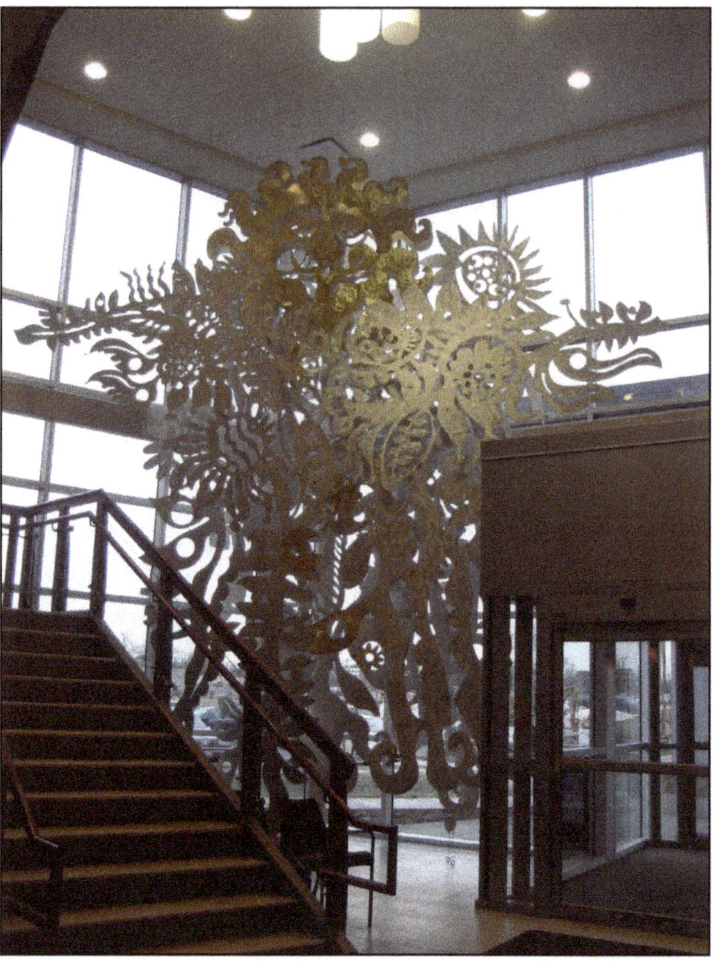

Garden of Fantasy

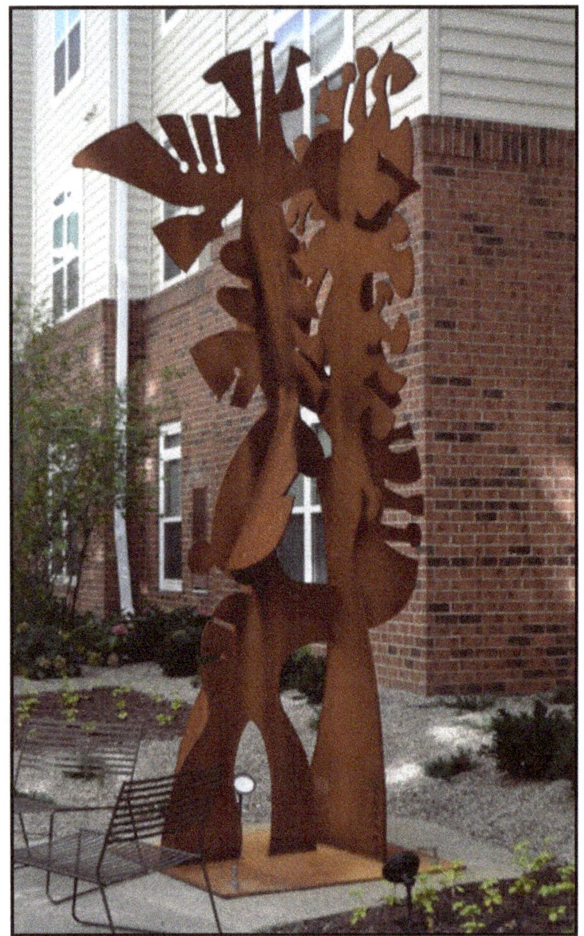

Akron's Edge Apartments. The University of Akron's Edge Apartments are COR-TEN.

images; abstract, where you may or may not recognize the object which has been transformed; and nonobjective, with no subject matter.

"You are dealing with the material of space, negative and positive. Negative: the space or area letting the light through; and positive: the material you see.

"I like to have a good idea of the environment. If it will be outdoors, I want some say on where it is going to be placed.

"I prefer to work with metals. Years ago, I worked more with cement, sandblasting into existing surfaces. Now that I am older I prefer to spend more time on the design rather than crawling up and down.

"I have formed a relationship with an artist studio in Durham, North Carolina, that does the fabrication work for me.

"Stainless or aluminum hold up very well with the largest pieces. COR-TEN, or all-weathering steel, is a favorite of mine. It appears rugged and ages over time from the original rust color to a deep purple-brown. COR-TEN is extremely stable in the environment for many years to come."

What would you say was the toughest piece you have done?

"No question about it—the Bowling Green University walls."

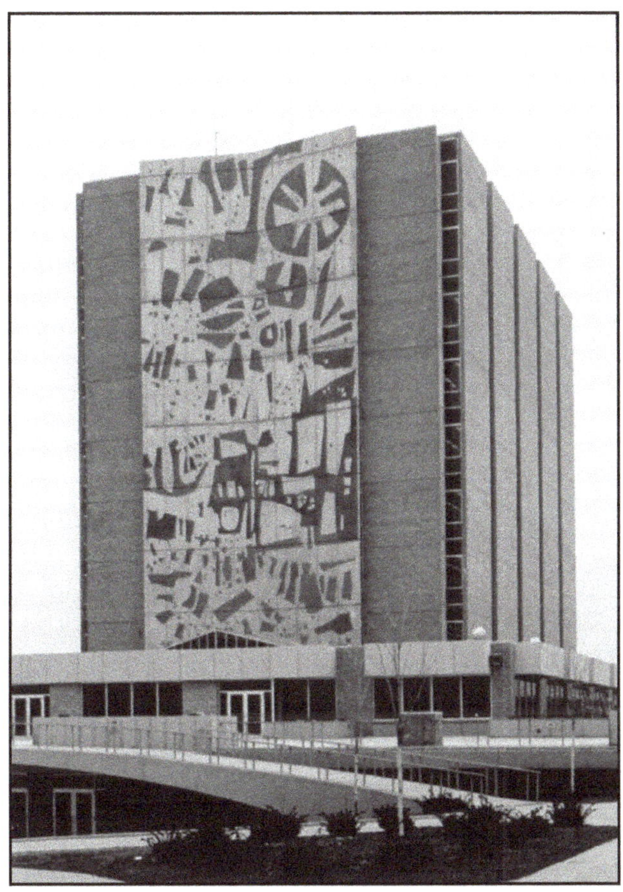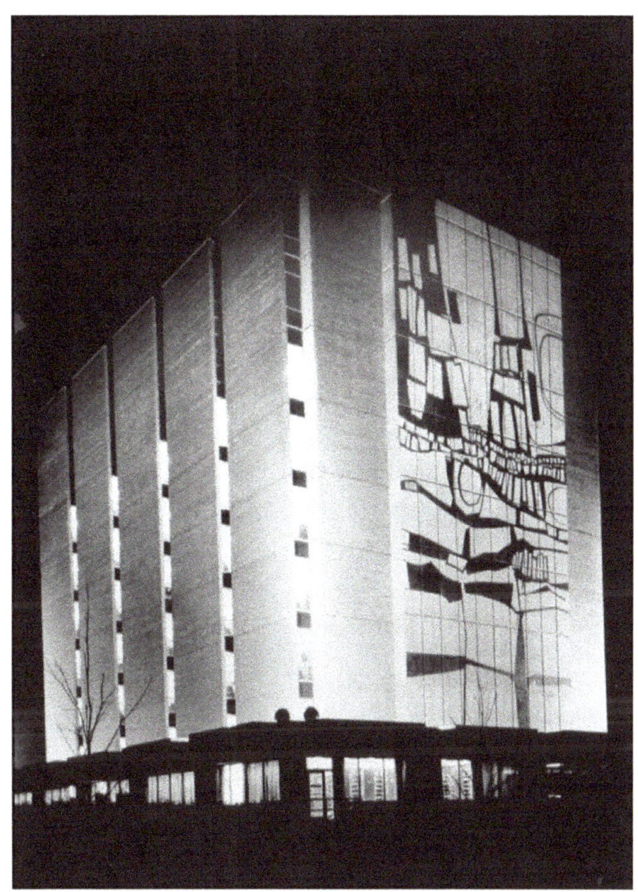

Bowling Green University Walls

"I designed both walls at either end of the building, one ten and one eight stories high. I was on scaffolding for days. I painted my designs directly onto the existing cement wall, using a small gridded map of my designs, and counting blocks as I went, in order to maintain the proper proportions. Sandblasters came behind me, cutting the design into the wall. Unfortunately, the aggregate in the cement was lighter than the surface cement, making the design very faint. This necessitated tinting the design. Painters were sent up to color the design, starting at the top, each carrying a bucket of material. Upon completion, I got a frantic call saying the color was strong at the top but very light at the bottom. I rushed to Bowling Green, took one look, and said, 'Did you give the painters sticks to stir the paint as they went down?' The color had settled to the bottom of the buckets. The wall had to be painted a second time."

"Kent State is my alma mater. The first COR-TEN piece I ever did was for Kent State. Kent wanted to bring in industrial art teachers in order to raise their level of creativity.

"With that in mind, I felt I could use them to assist in creating the COR-TEN sculpture. This sculpture went up in 1967.

"May 4, 1970, is the painful date of the Kent State shootings. The students were protesting President Nixon's sending bombings into Cambodia.

"The governor of Ohio sent the National Guard into Kent to control the protestors. Four students were killed. One student died right near my sculpture. I was asked to come to Kent and look at the sculpture because it was pierced by a bullet hole. The bullet hole looked like it came from the student angle. The National Guard stated they were fired on first. *The Akron Beacon Journal* took me up there. I looked at the hole and it looked concave and splayed out. I had taken a piece of metal with me and we took it to a farm and we fired into it. The bullet hole definitely came from the Guardsman, not the students. This was based on the trajectory of the bullet and its effect on the metal.

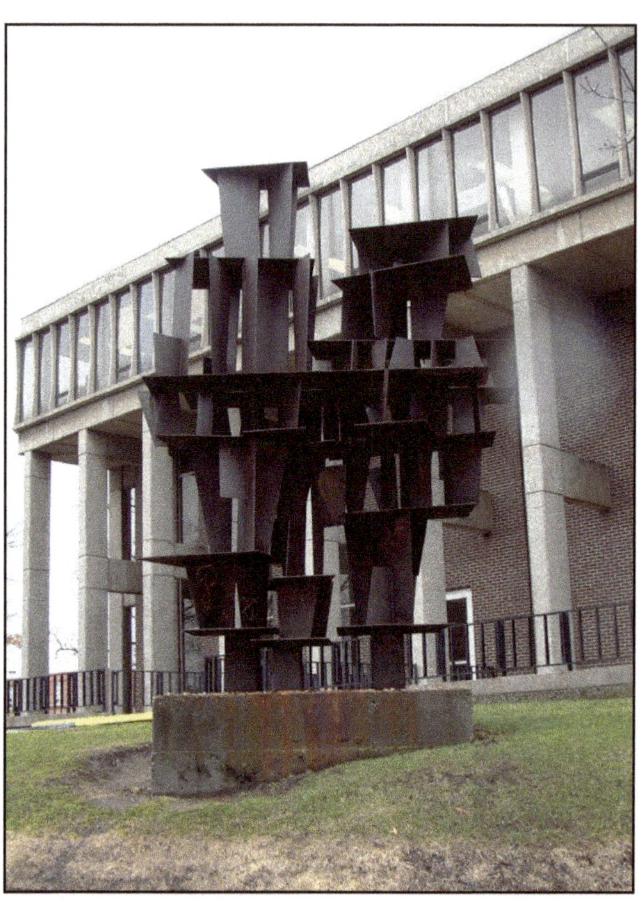

Kent State

"Bowling Green requested that I also create a memorial to the Kent State shootings. I called that one *Bridge over Troubled Water.*"

Quaker Oats were once produced in Akron, Ohio, but the company moved, leaving behind an empty factory and the silos for the grain. Developers decided to convert the silos into a hotel, a unique concept at the time. Don was commissioned to create murals for the public areas of the hotel. He used the sgraffito technique of applying cement plaster in layered colors and then cutting and scraping down through the surfaces to reveal his design. He also used gears rescued from the old factory throughout the murals, several depicting Akron's past industry.

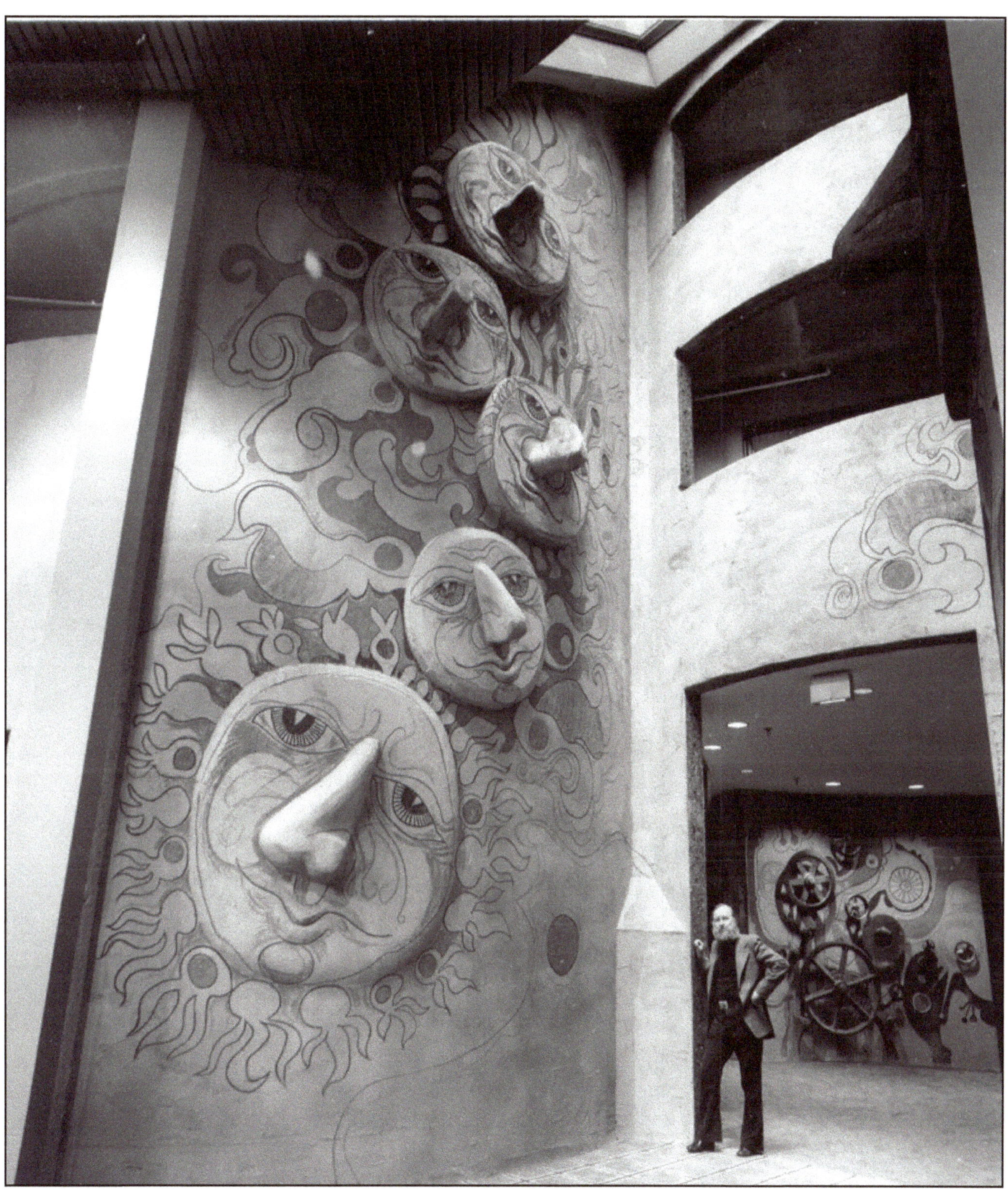

Quaker Oats Silos

"I was called to do a school in East Tennessee. Miss Rose was my contact there, a very interesting woman. I told them that I would do this project for them, all I wanted was for the organization to supply all the materials for the job. When it was completed, they invited me back and they presented me with a brown bag. They said, Enjoy! It was a bottle of White Lighting. It was mean stuff and I think I still have some to this day."

What work, of the hundreds you have done, is your favorite?

"The next one."

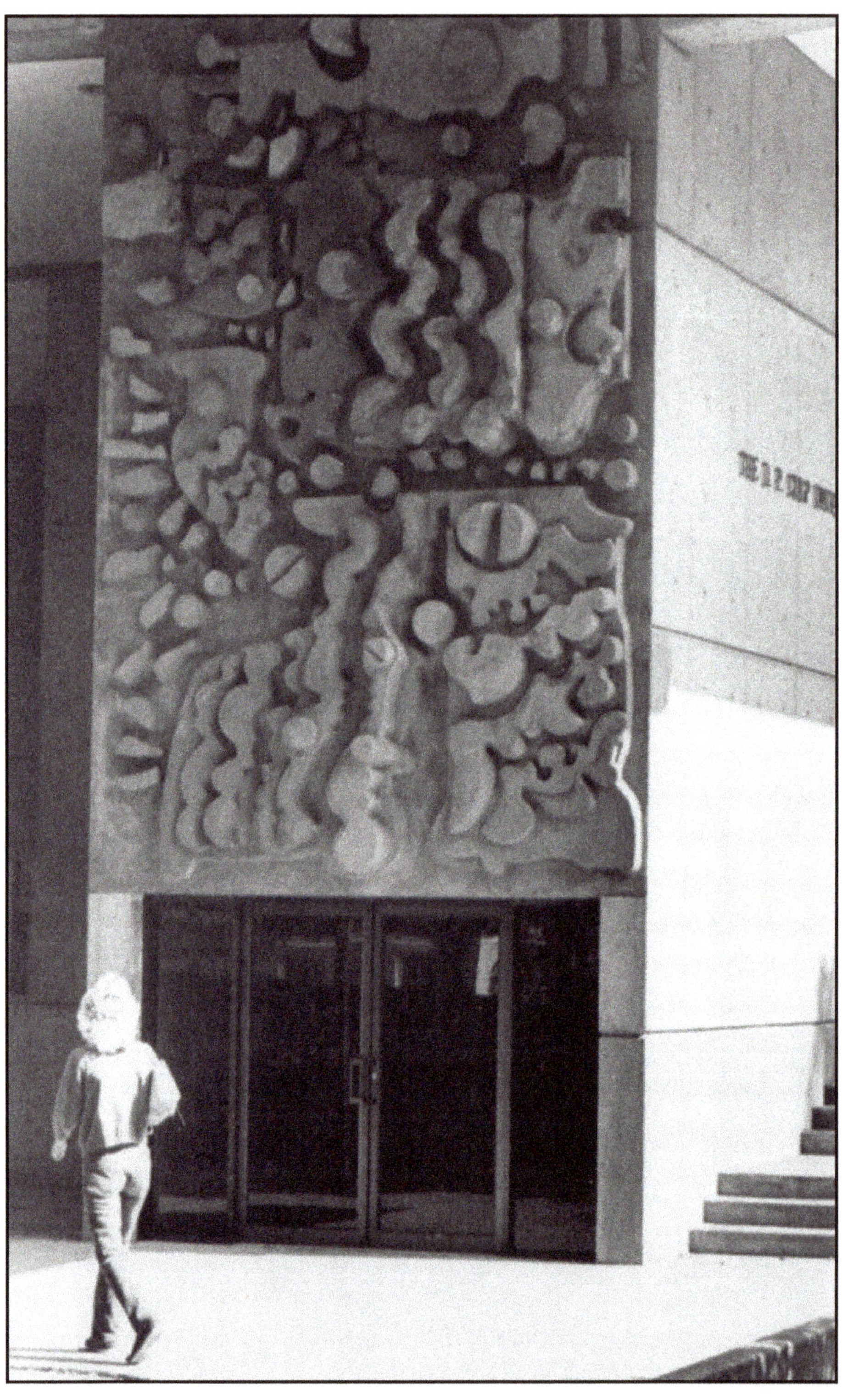

East Tennessee School

Don Drumm has received numerous awards. A few are listed below:

- Ohio Designer Crafts Lifetime Achievement Award
- The Akron Beacon Journal Publishing Company's Outstanding Contributors of the Century award
- Akron Area Arts Alliance in 2000, first recipient of the Outstanding Visual Artist Award
- First recipient of the American Institute of Architecture (AIA) Artist and Craftsman Excellence Award
- Summit County Historical Society presented Don and Lisa Drumm the Summit Award 2015. This award honored the Drumms' distinguished contribution and excellence in American crafts in the Greater Akron area and beyond.

"First Night" in Akron, Ohio, is a New Year's Eve event, and Don Drumm designed the very first button for the event in 1996, and the 2016 button for its 20th anniversary celebration. First Night is a family-friendly event and this past year Drumm designed a fun and cheerful button. The buttons are part of a cultural event well known for its enhancement of the Arts in Akron.

Don now feels these past five to six years have seen his best work. Taking on back-to-back commission work had been wonderful over the past couple of years. As Don claims emphatically, "I plan on working until I physically can't."

> *"Each object you do—you never feel it is complete in itself. It is a stepping stone on a road that never ends."*
>
> — *Don Drumm*

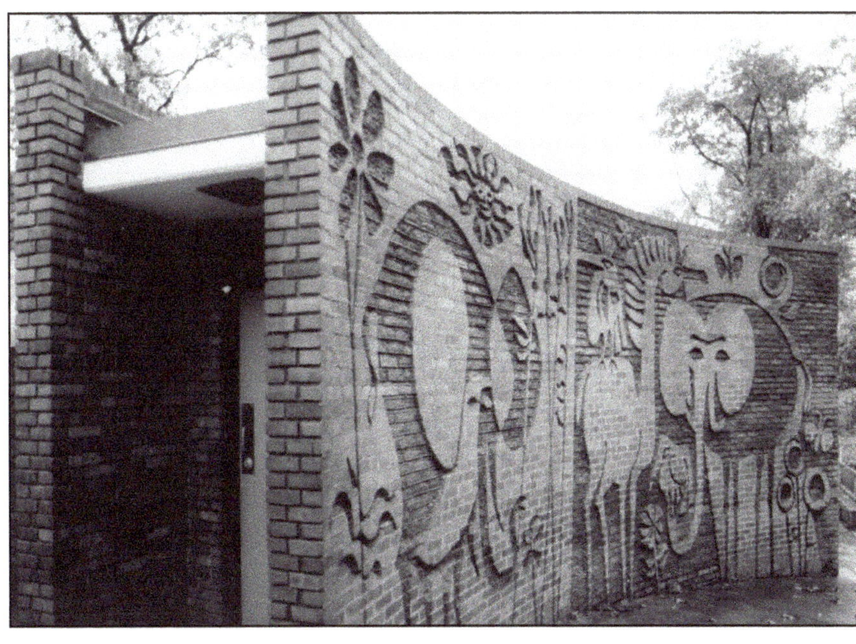

The Akron Zoo displays the fanciful animals sandblasted into cement on a brick wall.

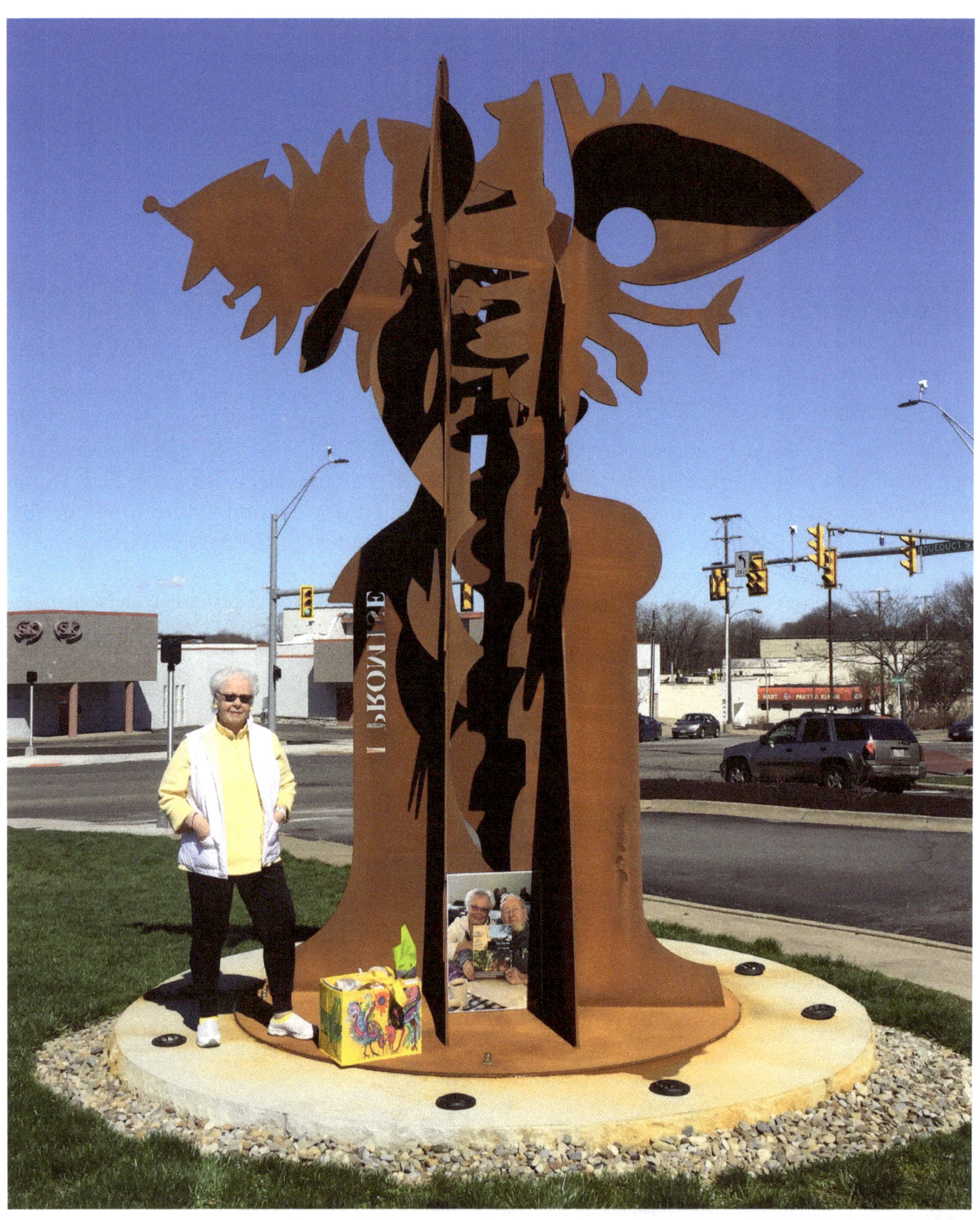

Drumm's custom Tree of Life statue adorns the front of the LeBron James Family Foundation's and Akron Public School's I PROMISE School. Greeting its guests with its towering features and abstract design, the piece serves to welcome and inspire the school's students and all who embark upon Akron's new model of urban education.

My Journey with Don Drumm

I would like to tell you how this whole book idea was actually birthed.

Let's go back to the Wadsworth Public Library in June of 2015. It was a wonderful summer evening, and we had read the notice Don Drumm was coming to lecture in Wadsworth, Ohio. My daughters and I have been admirers of Don Drumm for years. We all have treasures of his craft purchased from our many shopping adventures, so I was really excited to hear Don Drumm speak. After Don had completed his presentation, quite a few in the audience approached Don with questions and comments.

My turn finally came. I wished Don a happy birthday. I asked Don if he had a book written about him at his studio. The reason I asked was because his presentation was so powerful, someone needed to tell the story. (While he was describing his structures, all I could think was: we are sitting in the presence of an icon.) Don responded, "No, no, I do not want to have anything to do with writing a book."

I continued, "But what you shared tonight is so amazing. How you have done what you have done to create these masterpieces—skyscrapers that reach for the heavens—is remarkable!"

Don paused for a moment, looked me squarely in my eyes, raised his finger, pointed it directly in my face, and said, "You write it!"

He then instructed me to see Lisa, who was sitting in the audience. I immediately approached her and shared what I had discussed with Don and what I would like to do: take him up on his challenge, write the book. Lisa said, "E-mail me." She was very inviting and warm. I was encouraged and thought, maybe this is an opportunity to launch something really new.

From that point on, the adventure became a challenge to follow a dream, a vision. I was electrified by his presentation, and for about a year it became my mission to accomplish this book. Throughout this year of discussions, clarifications, and dream sharing, Lisa never doubted my vision. She was a shining star throughout. I felt like we had known each other for years. Her infectious sense of humor was contagious.

A one-year journey culminated with a noon meeting with Lisa and Mary (Don's photographer), and Don eventually joining us. The book will be written by me. I had waited over a year to hear that go-ahead.

Don said, "So when do we begin?" I said, "I am off Fridays." He said, "How about tomorrow?" I said, "Let's go." That became the nucleus of this edition before you. Little did I know what an incredible time I was in for.

In all reality, I feel like I have been in a space warp time capsule, maybe even dreaming this. It cannot be really happening, can it? So many with whom that I have shared this possibility have inquired, "How did this happen? How did you meet Don Drumm? Where did it start?" I have journaled the adventure, and would like to share that next.

Friday, DAY ONE

He described his lean beginnings while emphasizing that an artist needs to marry a woman with a job! (His words held time and space in the palm of his hands.) His hands are chiseled with art; they should be bronzed. They hold within them his life's blood of history, erected again and again throughout cities, hospitals, villages, landscapes, and homesteads.

Don has so much compassion for his work, but even more importantly he is a true humanitarian. The two hours flew by in a flash, and as we wrapped it up I wasn't sure if I would have any other opportunity to meet with him until he said, "When do we meet again?"

Friday, DAY TWO

Mary (photographer for the studio) texted me on Wednesday and told me to be ready on Friday, Don wanted to take us to lunch. I really felt like I was with a celebrity, so where in Don's world will he take us? Little again would I have ever guessed how special the eatery would be.

The café was first on the agenda. Mary, Don, and I were off to eat. It is so interesting to listen to Don narrate the surrounding building structures and the changes going on and all the establishments that he supports in the city. We passed a barbershop he frequents at least twice a year for $7.00, and a $3.00 tip, good deal! He is so real all the time. His suspenders, jeans, and seasoned shirt are all Don; and he jingles, just like my grandpa did, with keys galore.

We arrived at the Front Porch Cafe. Don raved about their mission: For many individuals, the Front Porch is a place where people gather as friend and family—just like the front porch of your home (www.SouthStreetMinistries.org).

As we approached, the cook, sitting outside, slipped into the café, ready to serve. They all knew Don. We were attended by a dear lady, a real Don fan. Don was served a place mat upside down. Guess why? Yep, he is always drawing, and they know that. Don asked for her cookies, but to his dismay all were gone. (Don likes cookies!) The Front Porch is a humble dwelling place to eat, warm with love oozing from every corner and from everyone sitting around. A true habitat for

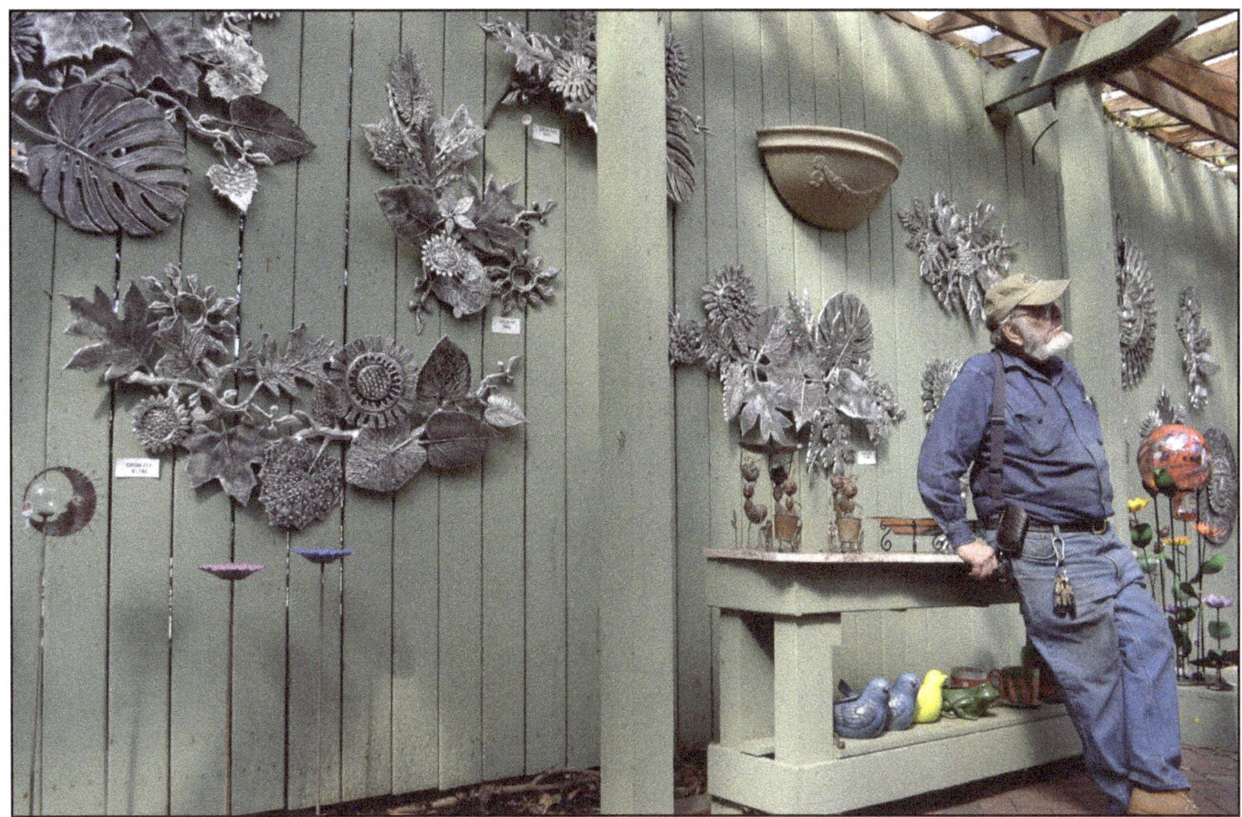

humanity to dwell in. That's Don. More than I can tell from all the hours thus far of listening to him, this is the true person. A man constantly looking for ways to help.

Mary recorded each session. These films will be logged into a treasure trove of history to follow in Don's legacy.

This session concentrated on his commissioned works and their stories. Don's tales of erecting the edifices reminded me of the original presentation at the Wadsworth Library.

I ended the session with a request to see Don's studio someday. Well, for Don, today WAS the day. Off we walked, Mary, Don, and I, to Don's personal studio. I was thinking of the area behind the Drumms Studio, but Don chose to take us to his private studio. Sam, Don's dog, greeted us warmly.

As we followed Don, I felt in awe again, as if traveling back in time. The narrow aisle we walked through revealed history; art, displayed, or tossed aside, unneeded. Then the sound of a radio, not loud, just enough to send sound bites into the air, maybe fifty or more years old. Preciously vintage.

Don then entered his favorite area. He has a bit of an unusual fancy for rats. YEP. They are really quite cute when you listen to Don share their story. Don took "Mister" out and coddled him, but "Mrs." was guarding her young brood. No messing with Mama. Mary loved filming this event. Then we were introduced to, I call her, "Salt 'n' Pepper," a special black-and-white rat. This one was very cute as she shimmied up the side of the cage and leaned her little nose over the edge, waiting for her keeper to pick her up. Don took her into his welcoming hands, where she seemed right at home. We then continued around and through another small area with another antique radio humming softly.

Then we entered THE area.

This was the pioneer's room. Almost a real Santa's workshop—with a weathered stool that knew comfort to the one and only. A box of metal pieces sat beneath the small table. The latest, truly handmade, creations of metal and everything else he can think of. His "CARS"—pieces of every size and shape welded together to create a keepsake for years to come. They even move on wheels, some even had more than four.

My heart held these moments as so special, hours that I will remember being honored to witness and now share with you.

Friday, DAY THREE

This time was a bit varied. I always shop when I visit the Gallery and discover something I had not seen before. This time I was able to tap Leona, assistant manager for the Gallery. Leona shared her admiration and amazement of Don and Lisa's ability to "go" like there is no tomorrow. Every day hard at work, ever caring about their studio, the customers, and the almost fifty staff members that support the Studio.

Don caught up with me, but Mary was off this particular Friday. Don continued his intriguing explanations of his commissions. His mind seeks out the wordless metals and shapes to exclaim his passion, his creativity.

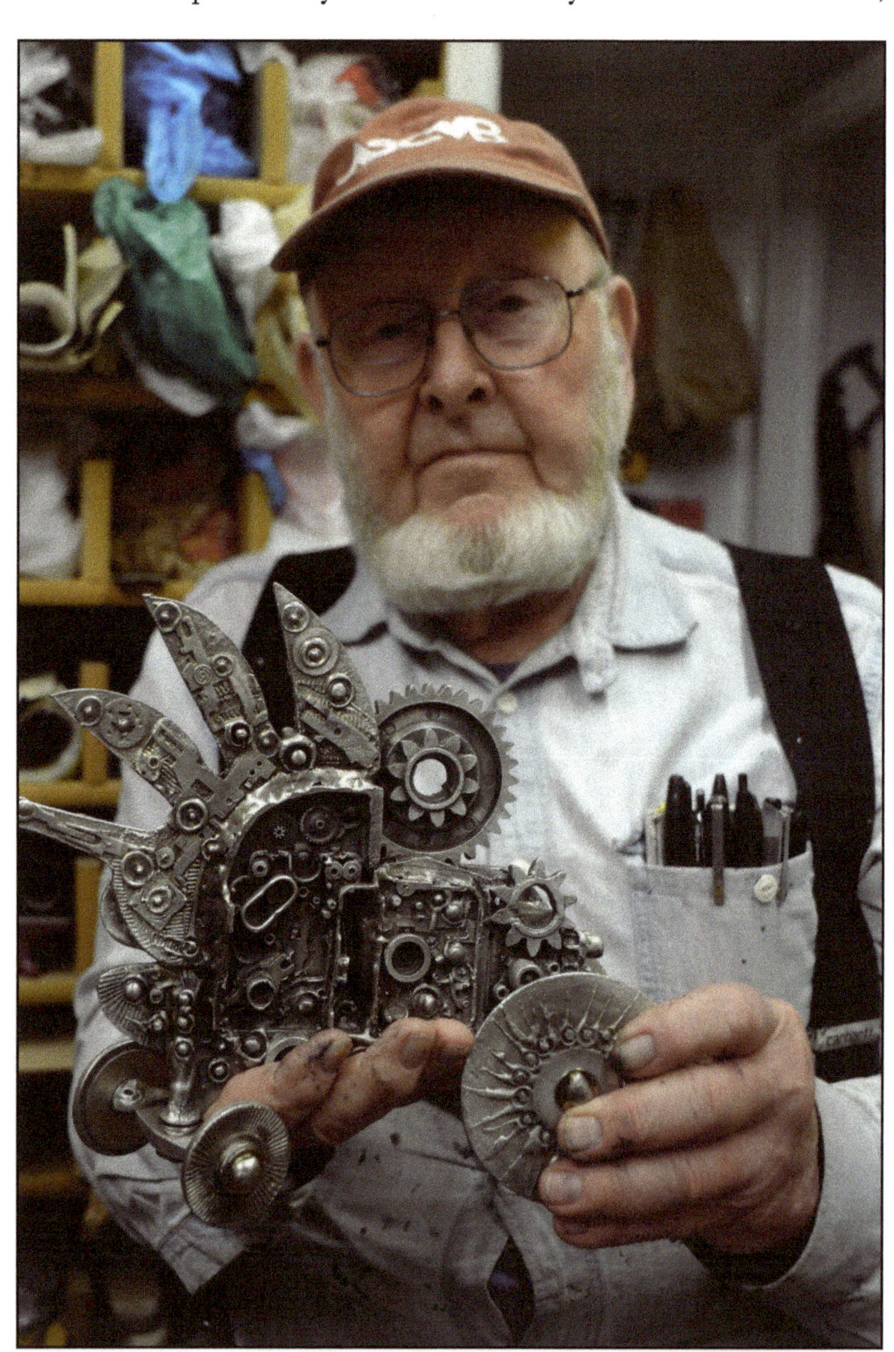

Can his work speak? Can it exclaim, "I have a mission, can you see it?" Maybe as the eyes behold magnificence and our hands want to reach out and touch the sculpture, they speak through their silence.

Once again, we wrapped up with Don saying, in his inevitable way with a lark in his voice, "Let's go to lunch." This time it was Fred's, another Akron inner-city great. A real Don restaurant. Everyone smiled and greeted Don and served us well. The place mat turned over, of course. Lunch was yummy, especially the mac and cheese.

At the close of this day, I exclaimed, "We'll have to do this again sometime." Don said, "I thought this was every Friday!" I chuckled, never dreaming it would be so. He also shared his sketchbook. I flipped though it in awe, feeling, yes, blessed to look through this window into the world of a master artist. A man of humility, strong convictions, and faith. A man faithful to life, his family, and his work.

Friday, DAY FOUR

This Friday, I called Don and asked him if my husband, Paul, could join us. Paul's career in the welding industry would be an added help in my understanding of how braze welding works, what a TIG welder is, etc.

As we sat down, Don spotted the bag of cookies and said, "Are those for me?" They were Paul's gift to Don.

 Don shared how he had sought out tradesmen—plasterers, bricklayers, sandblasters, and welders— in the beginning of his career, to learn as much as he could from them. Every one of them combined to initiate and bring reality to his art.

Lunchtime was in order. I think this is Don's favorite time. We ventured off to the Front Porch and had a wonderful time catching up with many friends of Don's. More tales of the mission and outreach successes.

Paul and I were both hopeful that we would be allowed to visit the workshop where the finishing touches take place, and we left with that in Don's court. He said, "Next Friday is okay!"

Friday, DAY FIVE

This visit was captured by Lisa. We were ushered into the Gallery and made our way to the first room; this is where all the pieces receive their finishing touches and are inspected and approved for the Gallery.

We proceeded to the workshop through the padded door. The padding is extremely helpful to quiet the sounds of machinery. The technicians were working on the polishing phase. One technician was holding a bowl and slowly letting the hanging sanding disc polish and smooth out the entire piece. Every inch of this workshop is taken up with machines, welders, or tools. The most fascinating instrument was the polishing machine (a vibratory polisher) that shines as it tosses the piece of art through ball bearings and frothing foam.

Lisa described the purpose of each machine's job and what each technician was doing. She knew it inside and out.

Don entered the workshop and posed a question: "Are we ready to eat?" The four of us made our way back through the wrapping station, and then Don stopped and asked, "Where are my cookies?" I had them ready, but the whole staff turned and said, "Cookies!" Don leaned to me and said, "Uh-oh. Guess I should have waited to ask." However, he grabbed them and said, "These are off to my office!"

(I would love to interject here and mention the absolutely stylish way that the gifts are wrapped at the Drumm Gallery. No ordinary wrapping. They are skillfully put in Bubble Wrap, taped galore, and placed artistically in colored tissue. The stylish bags are then wrapped with ribbons of appropriate color, curled and strung with a gift card attached. NO CHARGE. This is what separates this gift gallery from all others: their attention to detail. No gift is too small to wrap.)

 The four of us headed to the Front Porch. We were welcomed by the warm crowd and shared our family stories in this real down-home atmosphere.

The story never really ends; it has actually only just begun….

My thanks to each of you for your interest in my journey. May this window into Don and Lisa Drumm's life cause you to pause and study the piece you may be holding in your hands and know it is a work of art. Each and every craft piece or wall piece is individually made to perfection.

Enjoy!

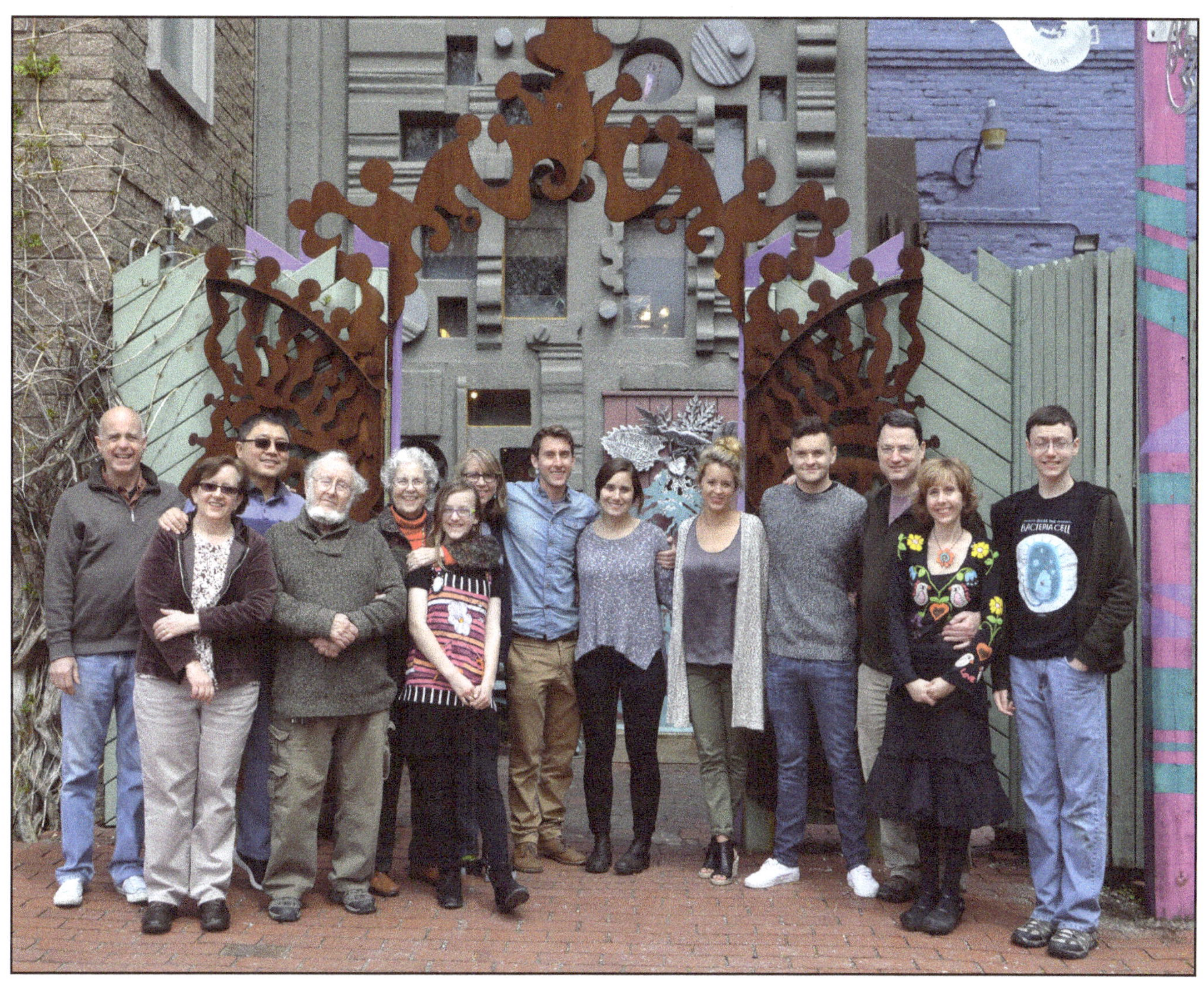

Front Row, left to right:
Tamula Drumm (daughter), Don Drumm, Andra Benninghoff (granddaughter), Leandra Drumm-Benninghoff (Daughter)

Back Row left to right:
Jeff VanAuken (Son-in-law), Xiaoming Song (Son-in-law), Lisa Drumm, Elisa Drumm VanAuken (Daughter), Cory VanAuken (Grandson), Amanda McManaway VanAuken (wife of Cory), Addison VanAuken Waters (Granddaughter), Oliver Waters (Husband of Addison), Tim Benninghoff (son-in-law), Logan Benninghoff (Grandson)

For more information on the Don Drumm Studio and Gallery,

visit: www.dondrummstudios.com

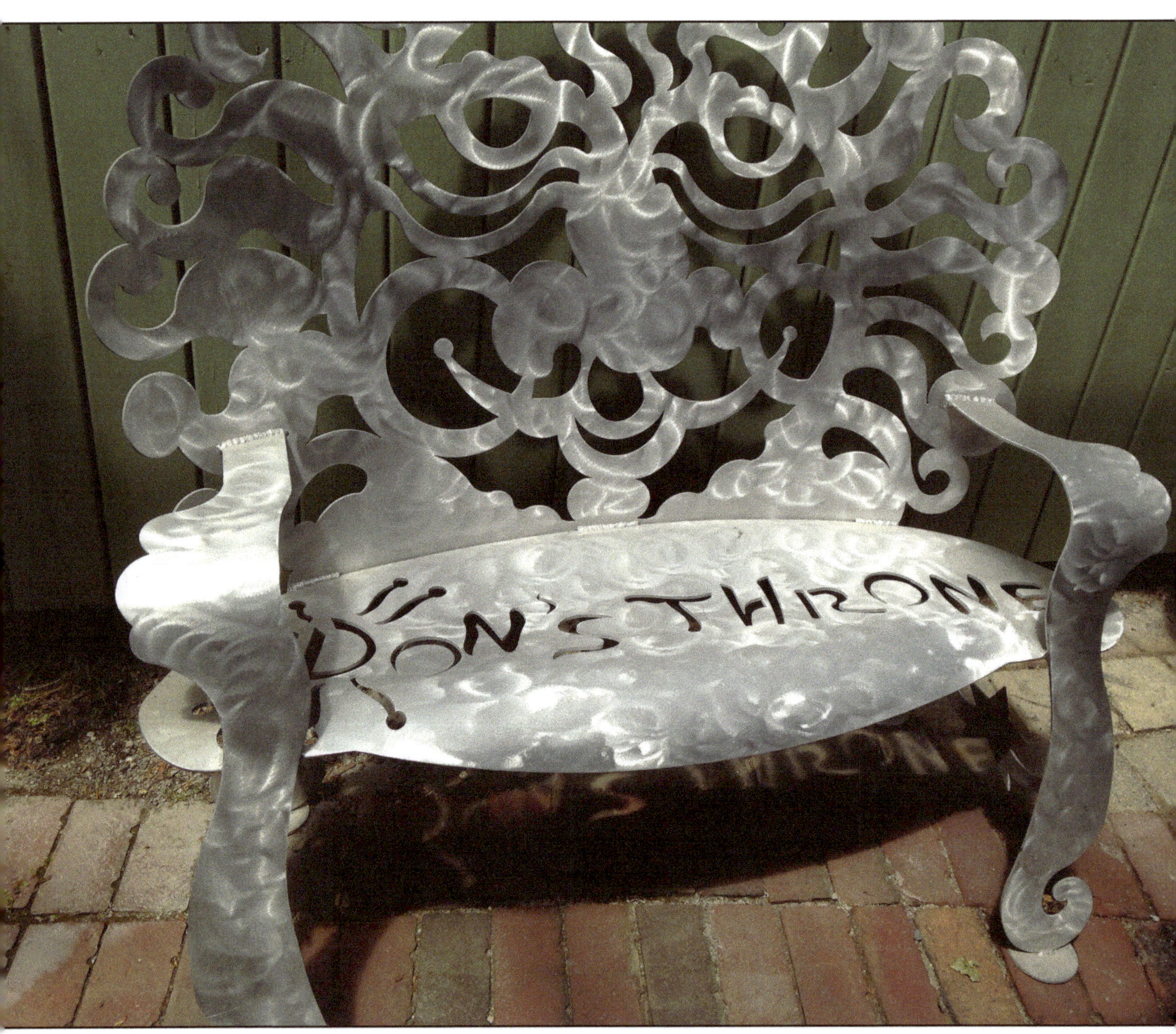
DON'S THRONE